INSIDER TIPS FOR HUNTING BIG GAME

XINA M. UHL
AND JUDY MONROE PETERSON

rosen publishing's
rosen
central

New York

Published in 2019 by The Rosen Publishing Group, Inc.
29 East 21st Street, New York, NY 10010

First Edition

Library of Congress Cataloging-in-Publication Data

Names: Uhl, Xina M., author. | Peterson, Judy Monroe, author.
Title: Insider tips for hunting big game / Xina M. Uhl and Judy Monroe Peterson.
Description: New York : Rosen Central, 2019. | Series: The ultimate guide to hunting | Audience: Grades 5–8. | Includes bibliographical references and index.
Identifiers: LCCN 2017048321 | ISBN 9781508181774 (library bound) | ISBN 9781508181781 (pbk.)
Subjects: LCSH: Big game hunting—Juvenile literature.
Classification: LCC SK35.5 .U35 2019 | DDC 799.2/6—dc23
LC record available at https://lccn.loc.gov/2017048321

Manufactured in the United States of America

CONTENTS

INTRODUCTION

Although humans have spread over the entire earth, regularly sail the high seas in massive supertankers, and build skyscrapers that soar hundreds of feet in the air, there is one thing we can't escape: our animal nature. Humans have been at the top of the food chain for thousands of years. Hunting for our food, matching wits against creatures that are intelligent and fast, and enjoying the great outdoors is in our blood.

North America's big game offer a worthwhile challenge to hunters. The large expanses of wilderness in Canada and the United States are home to white-tailed deer, mule deer, moose, elk, bear, and wild boar. They live in forests, near lakes and rivers, in mountains, foothills, grasslands, deserts, and high plains. Deer are the most abundant of the big game animals, and their herds are often in need of culling so that their numbers don't overtax natural resources and lead to starvation.

Hunting allows individuals, sometimes together with friends and family, to explore nature, spend time outdoors in physical and mental exercise, observe wildlife, and harvest delicious meat. The quiet of the woods is welcome to many people who live in loud, busy cities and towns, so much so that hunting can be rewarding and enjoyable even if the hunter does not return home having harvested an animal.

Animals typically live in rugged, well-concealed land, challenging hunters to walk miles to find them and then expend energy carrying or dragging a heavy carcass back to their campsite or vehicle. Physical endurance can be tested.

Meat from big game animals has many advantages over meat from the grocery store. It is lean, nutritious, healthy, and tasty.

A Rocky Mountain bull elk has the largest antlers of all elk sub-species. Bulls weigh an average of 700 pounds (315 kilograms) while cows average 500 pounds (225 kg).

Other parts of the animal are used as well. These include the hides, fur, bones, or horns, all of which are used to make clothing, shoes, boots, belts, jewelry, handbags, and other accessories.

Camaraderie is another important part of hunting. Family or friends may gather together year after year in the same area to hunt big game. They enjoy the companionship and the chance to bond with one another. Hunting skills are passed down through the generations in many families. The sport, fun, relaxation, and time spent outdoors makes for good times. Hunters may preserve and display animals they kill.

The management and conservation of wildlife and natural habitats is very important for hunters, who help to balance wild-

Many families enjoy spending time in nature during hunting trips, whether or not their hunts are successful.

life populations. Big game hunters must follow laws and regulations and respect practices that protect endangered animals. Hunters support wildlife management and conservation programs by paying for licenses and special taxes on hunting equipment. Most states do not have other ways to raise money for conservation. Hunters also often donate their time to help with wildlife management projects like developing food and shelter habitats.

In order to successfully, safely hunt big game, every hunter needs proper training. It is essential for hunters to learn how to handle and shoot firearms and archery properly. Hunters must know the laws and what their responsibilities are before, during, and after a hunt. Other skills necessary are planning, outdoor skills like orienteering, and knowledge about wildlife and environments to hunt big game.

CHAPTER ONE

LEARNING THE BASICS

I n order to make their way through forests and other terrain and hunt wild, sometimes dangerous, animals, hunters need basic hunting skills and knowledge. It's important for hunters to have a thorough understanding of the workings of their weapons, in particular the rifle, which most hunters use when going after large animals. Rifles and other weapons used for big game hunting, such as slug shotguns, muzzleloaders, and bows and arrows, come with different styles and types of ammunition depending on their usage.

HUNTING EDUCATION

Beginning hunters need to learn the safe and correct use of weapons, including handling, transporting, and carrying while they are hunting. They often learn skills from family members or friends who pass the knowledge down through generations. Most states require beginning hunters to take an official state training program. A state's natural resources or conservation department typically offers hunter education classes. After completing and passing the course, beginning hunters can then buy a hunting license. Conservation and shooting clubs also offer

A rifle is a firearm with a rifled bore, or special grooves cut into the barrel in order to spin the bullet when it is fired, allowing for improved accuracy over nonrifled bores.

hunter education classes and seminars before the start of each hunting season. Important classes are firearm safety, proper use of firearms, archery, regulations, and animal identification.

Whether using firearms or archery, hunters need to be on the mark when shooting. They want to harvest an animal, not wound it or miss and scare it away. Becoming a good shot requires a lot of practice with a firearm or bow and arrow. Good hunters spend time at a target range shooting at practice targets to become familiar with their weapon. Most shooting ranges have outdoor and indoor targets. Beginning shooters aim at targets that are placed at close range. As they advance, they shoot at targets at longer ranges. Hunters can read books and

As with any new endeavor, practice is essential to mastering shooting skills. This shooter's position mimics possible hunting conditions.

go to websites for information about the safe use of weapons for hunting large animals. All hunters need to know the laws and responsibilities of hunting.

FIREARM PURCHASING

The federal government controls all laws on buying firearms, but different states may have different restrictions on firearm purchases. The age of the firearm buyer is restricted. A parent or guardian must buy and register the firearm for young (underage) hunters. Each state controls the big game season and what type of weapons can be

SAFETY MUSTS FOR WEAPONS

Every state in the United States offers a hunting safety program. Most states require beginning hunters to take this class before their first hunt. The following are some of the important rules for the safe handling of weapons. Always assume a firearm is loaded and handle it carefully. Keep a firearm unloaded until you are ready to use it. When carrying a firearm, open the action, keep your fingers away from the trigger, and keep the safety switch on. A safety can fail, so do not assume the safety will always work. Only point a weapon at the target and in a safe direction. Do not fire at only sound or movement or where hunters or other people might be. Never lean a firearm against a tree, rock, fence, or other object as it could fall and accidentally fire. Because firearms make loud noises and release debris (fragments), a hunter should wear ear protectors and shooting glasses when he or she is on a shooting range or hunting. After using firearms, store them and the ammunition separately in safe and secure places.

used and when. Some areas with flat land or farmland restrict hunters to a particular gun, which is usually a slug shotgun. Compared to those from a shotgun, bullets from rifles travel farther.

USING RIFLES

Before using a rifle, a hunter should consider how it fits and its weight, size, action, and caliber. A rifle that is too long or too short will be uncomfortable to hold and use. Most rifles for hunting big game weigh between 6 and 9 pounds (2.7 to 4.1 kg). Although lighter rifles are more comfortable to carry, heavier rifles recoil (kick back) less. In addition, heavier rifles are easier to hold steady and are better for stand hunting and shooting long range.

Many big game hunters use scopes on their rifles. A scope is a small telescope that is mounted on top of a rifle. Hunters line up the crosshairs (guides) on the scope to aim accurately and be more precise with their shot. The magnification of a scope allows them to see an animal better than with the unaided eye. A typical scope uses three times (3X) magnification. This means that an animal appears three times closer than it does without the scope.

Rifle scopes allow hunters to see targets in the distance, improving the accuracy of their shots.

Rifles are made to shoot a specific caliber of bullet. The larger the caliber is, the larger the bullet. The long, thin barrel of a rifle increases the accuracy of the lead bullet as it is fired. The precision is due to the grooves that twist around inside the barrel. The grooves cause bullets to spin as they move through the barrel. The spin helps stabilize bullets, which increases their accuracy and allows them to travel great distances.

Many rifle models with different actions are available. The most common model for hunting large wildlife is a bolt action in which the bolt is operated by hand. Many people think the bolt action is the most reliable and accurate rifle. Other popular rifle actions are pump, break, semiautomatic, and lever. Hunters often choose an action depending on where they will hunt. For example, high-powered rifles with bolt actions and good scopes are the best choice in wide-open spaces for long-distance shooting. Semi-automatic action rifles are typically used when fast-moving large animals are the target. Some hunters prefer lever or pump actions in wooded areas or if they walk while hunting.

Most states have laws that specify the minimum bullet caliber (diameter size) for big game hunting. The most common bullet sizes for rifles are .30-30, .270, .30-06, and .308. Many big game hunters think that the .30-06 is the most versatile. These bullets travel 1 mile (1.6 km) or more and shoot accurately at up to 300 yards (274 m). A rifle's caliber is stamped on its barrel.

USING HANDGUNS, SLUG SHOTGUNS, AND MUZZLELOADERS

A shotgun has a long, smooth barrel. For hunting big game, people use a shotgun that shoots slugs. Two popular slugs are the sabot and the Foster. The sabot slug has a long, slender shape. The Foster slug looks like a cup with twisted grooves on the outside. The grooves cause the bullet to spin, increasing its precision and distance. The 12-gauge slug shotgun is the most popular.

Some hunters like using muzzleloaders, also called black powder guns. These guns are loaded by putting black powder and a lead bullet into the muzzle, which are pressed down the barrel. The first shot must be a good one because reloading can take more than a minute. Hunters can choose muzzleloading shotguns and rifles. The most popular muzzleloading rifles for big game are 50 or 54 caliber. Many states have extended seasons for muzzleload hunting of big game.

Hunting large wildlife with a handgun or revolver takes great skill. Hunters must get close to an animal to make an accurate shot. Handguns that are single cartridge, five or six cartridges, and semiautomatic are available. Some handgun hunters mount a scope on the short barrel.

HUNTING WITH BOWS

Bowhunting, or shooting arrows with bows, is popular with many large wildlife hunters. People who shoot with a bow and arrow are called bowhunters or archers. It takes strength and special skills to bowhunt well. Hunters must build up the muscles that are required to shoot a bow. Compared to hunters using rifles, archers need to get much closer to an animal to shoot because arrows do not travel as far as bullets. It is more difficult to accurately shoot large wildlife using a bow and arrow than with a firearm. In many states, bowhunters can hunt for a longer period of time than those who use firearms.

For big game, hunters use a compound bow or a recurve bow. The compound bow is the most popular. It is made up of a system of strings, wheels, and pulleys that reduces the amount of force needed to hold the bow while it is drawn and ready for

Hunting using bows and arrows is one of the most ancient of human activities. Today's equipment is usually not handmade, however.

release. Hunters like this bow because it increases their control while they wait for the right moment to shoot. The recurve bow curves back against its natural bend, which gives it great power when the arrow is released. Some hunters prefer the recurve bow because it is lighter and quieter to shoot than the compound bow.

The correct bow to use for big game depends on the strength and size of a hunter. Bows are rated in pounds to pull the string back. For example, a bow rated at 50 pounds (23 kg) requires 50 pounds (23 kg) of force (strength) to pull back the string to draw an arrow. By increasing the force when pulling on a bow's string, the archer can send the arrow faster and farther.

Bowhunters who hunt large animals use the broadhead arrow. This arrow has two or more very sharp steel blades. A mechanical or expandable blade broadhead arrow expands when it hits something, which then exposes the blades. Many states have laws that specify the diameter and number of blades for broadhead arrows to use when hunting big game. The key skill for a bowhunter to master is the exact placement of an arrow tipped with a broadhead.

CHAPTER TWO

TO PROTECT AND CONSERVE

P ublic land, water, and wildlife are precious resources. Hunters have the duty to protect, conserve, and improve them whenever and wherever possible. Each state or province has laws designed to keep hunting safe, fair, and beneficial for humans and wildlife alike. Hunters must be careful to follow these laws in order to make the experience good for everyone involved.

PRIVATE AND PUBLIC LANDS

Hunters must know where it is legal to hunt wild animals. At all times, they must honor private property without trespassing. Hunting on private land without permission when it is posted with No Trespassing or No Hunting signs is a crime.

If they are allowed to hunt on private property, hunters need to be respectful of and responsible to landowners. What follows are some rules to abide by. Always ask landowners permission to hunt big game on their lands, and thank them when the hunting is done. Treat private land, farm animals, crops, and equipment carefully. After a successful hunt, it is a

17

NOTICE

The properties along this road do not allow public hunting on them. Trespassers will be prosecuted.

Property owners have the law on their side when it comes to trespassing, especially if they have posted signs like this one to warn hunters off their land.

good idea to offer landowners some of the meat. If they do not want the meat, come back and help them work with their crops or livestock, for example. By being respectful, hunters are often welcomed back each year by these people.

National and state forests are public lands. They are owned by all citizens. Big game hunters who are on public property have a duty to treat the land and campgrounds with care and keep the area clean by not littering. Furthermore, they can pick up litter that others have left behind. However hunters can demonstrate their goodwill is positive for the image of hunting as a whole.

LAWS AND REGULATIONS

Hunters need to follow federal and state laws that regulate the harvesting of big game animals. By law, hunters must shoot only specified weapons during an established season. They must harvest only the big game animals that are permissible. Most types of hunting have a season when it is legal to harvest each type of big game animal. Laws that manage the hunting of big game conserve wildlife by protecting the land from animals grazing to the point where they damage the vegetation and land cover. This overgrazing can harm the animals, too, by causing them to lose their main source of food. These hunting laws guarantee the privilege to hunt. Authorities closely watch big game in all states. To enforce hunting laws, states run registration stations and require hunters to possess game tags on the harvested animals.

Most states require underage hunters to pass a hunting course and then obtain a hunting certificate. The department of natural resources certifies this hunter education course. The course covers firearms and hunting safety, transporting and carrying firearms, and the basics of shooting. Beginners also learn about hunting responsibility, preparedness, and wildlife conservation and identification. To complete the course, students must pass a written test and show safe firearm handling skills. They then receive a certificate.

For positive identification, most states require hunters to have their hunter's certificate or driver's license in their possession. In some states, hunters are expected to wear a back tag (a tag attached to the back of their outer clothing) that displays their license number. The back tag provides personal identification. During the season, hunters must follow strict limits on the number of animals they can take. They must buy a license for each deer, elk, moose, bear, or wild boar (wild pig) that they want to

Hunting licenses come in different forms depending on where you are hunting. These are from the Division of Fisheries and Wildlife in Massachusetts.

hunt. Hunters can renew their hunting license to keep it current. Depending on the state, a license may be valid for days, one year, or other periods of time.

PUTTING ON A GOOD FACE

It is important for responsible hunters to show a positive image by being courteous and using common sense. Nonhunters and other hunters form opinions about big game hunters based on the big game hunters' actions. Hunters might meet other people enjoying the land and wildlife, such as hikers, bird watchers, and

ETHICS AND HUNTING

Sometimes problems come up that are not covered by federal or state laws. Being a responsible hunter means making decisions and doing things the right way even when no one is watching. Ethics refers to personal decisions beyond what the law requires. An ethical hunter is fair and respectful to animals, property, other hunters, and other people. Hunters follow a personal code, or a set of acceptable behaviors. A hunter's code is as important as hunting laws.

For example, some people think that they can hunt big game whenever they want. They might harvest wildlife outside of its season or during the season without following the regulations. Moreover, they might hunt without a license or game tags and harvest an animal. This illegal hunting is called poaching. When they are caught, the poachers will be fined. In most cases, they will lose their hunting privileges for years. They may also lose their hunting weapon, boats, and any motorized vehicle that was used when they poached.

skiers. Responsible hunters do not want to frighten or offend people who are afraid of firearms or who do not approve of hunting. When they aren't hunting, responsible hunters keep firearms unloaded, in cases, and stored out of sight.

To be responsible, hunters must obey the laws involving big game. They need to know their rifle or archery equipment, how it works, and how to shoot accurately. Hunters must know where to aim and how to hit a deer, moose, elk, bear, or wild boar for a fast and humane kill. They need to keep improving their shooting skills with weapons so that they do not wound their target. They can do this by practicing, taking classes, and learning from other hunters. If someone in the hunting group wounds an animal, track or help others to track it and recover the injured animal. When traveling from the hunting area, make sure to cover the harvested animal so it does not offend non-hunters.

Responsible hunters practice fair chase. They do not take unfair advantage of big game animals. For instance, hunters should not harvest an animal while it is eating illegal bait. Hunters are responsible for reading and following the state's definition of legal bait. Nor should they shoot an animal that is fenced in and cannot escape a hunter.

Hunters have a responsibility to make full use of the big game that they harvest. They should eat the meat. If they want to share harvested big game, they need to check the state regulations before offering meat to others. Some states provide ways for successful hunters to donate their big game animal to a local food bank. Many hunters like to take photos of their harvested big game. It is a good idea to make sure the photos are tasteful so that nonhunters are not offended when they look.

FELLOW HUNTERS DEPEND ON YOU

Big game hunters are responsible to all other hunters. Being safe is of utmost importance. Hunters expect one another to obey hunting laws and to respect hunting areas and zones of fire. The area in which a hunter can shoot safely is known as the zone of fire. When hunting alone, a hunter can shoot in any direction once the target and what is beyond it is clearly identified. However, a big game hunter must check that other hunters are not sharing the same hunting area.

Hunting in groups can be dangerous. Keep a keen eye out for your fellow hunters to prevent injury or death.

When hunting in groups, it is important that each hunter knows exactly where he or she can shoot and not put partners in danger. Hunting partners need to talk to set up the zone of fire for each other before they begin to shoot.

Even when partners have established their range of fire, more than one hunter might shoot at and harvest the same animal. Then they need to make a responsible decision as to who tags the big game. One decision might be that they agree to share the meat.

WILDLIFE BENEFITS FROM HUNTING

By law, big game hunters pay annual license and tag fees for the animals they want to hunt. Hunters also pay state and local taxes on hunting equipment. Funding of wildlife programs comes from these fees and taxes. Many types of wildlife, including wildlife that is not hunted, benefit from these management programs. Every year, hunting organizations across the nation raise millions of dollars for restoring or improving animal habitats, wildlife research, and education.

Deer and other wild animals have fur that can blend into the brush, making them difficult to spot.

Hunters need to know and promote wildlife conservation programs that guarantee stable wildlife populations for both hunters and nonhunters to enjoy. If an animal population gets too small and is in danger of becoming extinct, the federal or state government declares it endangered. It is illegal to hunt endangered animals. One of the main reasons that animal populations decline is because people use the animal's habitat. Local and national hunting associations work together with conservation organizations to protect wildlife, such as setting aside large pieces of wild land to conserve habitats. When hunters follow hunting seasons and limits, they are respecting conservation efforts. They leave enough members of an animal population to guarantee a future stable population.

On the other hand, if a wildlife population, such as that of the white-tailed deer, gets too large, the animals cannot find enough food or water. They might eat most or all of certain plants in an area, which ruins the plant environment. A plant environment that is overgrazed will lead to the animal population starving, moving to a new area, or becoming extinct. If starving, the animals might get sick and infect other wild animals with disease. Hunters help by thinning or reducing deer, wild boars, or other large animals overpopulating an area. Before beginning a hunt, hunters who plan ahead are more likely to have success.

CHAPTER THREE

IT'S TIME TO PLAN!

Do you want to have a safe, successful, enjoyable hunt? Of course you do. That takes one essential thing: planning ahead. When hunting big game, it's necessary to study the animal's behavior and habitat. It's also crucial to locate an appropriate place to hunt. Along with this knowledge, proper preparation with firearms—including practice shooting targets—allows for the most effective experience.

LEARNING ABOUT ANIMALS

All big game animals live where the plants that they eat are available, usually in forests and on mountains and along streams and lakes. Big game animals gather much information through their keen senses of smell and hearing. Deer, for example, can detect a person who is many blocks away by smelling. Most game animals do not travel far to find food and water. However, moose, elk, and bear will go long distances to search for food if necessary. These large animals require a lot of food to stay healthy. When hunters can find where animals feed, their success at harvesting big game increases greatly.

26

Moose are the largest members of the deer family. Their antlers can span up to 6 feet (1.8 meters) from end to end.

HOOFED MAMMALS

Deer, moose, and elk are members of the deer family. They have cloven hoofs with two parts, antlers that shed every year, and brown coats that blend in with their surroundings. Their diet is grass and low-growing plants such as clover, tree leaves, buds, and acorns. They also feed on almost any farm crop.

White-tailed deer are the number-one big game animal in North America. They are found in all fifty states and much of Canada. Most live along forest edges and brushy, low woodlands. Mule deer inhabit the western third of North America in brushy areas, forests, desert shrubs, and rock uplands. Deer often

Wild boars, like this one, can live up to ten years in the wild. They have been known to survive up to twenty-five years in captivity.

outsmart hunters with their amazing ability to disappear. When they sense danger, deer quickly find an escape path or a patch of cover. Fast runners, deer can reach 35 to 40 miles per hour (56 to 64 kilometers per hour) for short distances and easily jump an obstacle 8 feet (2.5 m) high. They are also strong swimmers. Mule deer have better vision than white-tailed deer. Of the more than two dozen varieties of white-tailed deer in North America, the largest is the northern white-tailed deer, which weighs up to 250 pounds (113 kg). Mule deer have large rabbitlike ears. The Rocky Mountain mule deer is the largest of the seven varieties, weighing up to 400 pounds (181 kg).

Moose inhabit the northern United States and most of Canada. They live in thick forests near shallow water. The lakes, marshes, and swamps provide a source of food. Like deer, moose are excellent swimmers and can run fast, up to 30 miles per hour (48 km/h). They have poorer sight than deer. Moose usually live by themselves. Elk are somewhat smaller than moose. A large male moose weighs 1,400 pounds (635 kg), and a large elk is about 1,100 pounds (499 kg). Although elks prefer grassy meadows, they will go to higher land or deep into a forest if danger approaches. Sometimes large herds, or groups, will move up to 100 miles (161 km) to find food. Elks trot long distances at 15 to 20 miles per hour (24–32 km/h), with bursts of speed of 35 miles per hour (56 km/h).

WILD BOARS AND BIG BEARS

Bears are intelligent game animals. Although they have poor eyesight, they have excellent senses of smell and hearing. Black bears are the most hunted variety of bear in much of the United States but are not common in the Midwest and Texas. They inhabit forests, swamps, and mountains. Like members of the deer family, bears eat grasses and crops. They also eat berries, fruits, nuts, insects, small animals, and fish. Bears are nimble, able to climb a tree in seconds, and can run 25 miles per hour (40 km/h) for short distances. Standing 5 to 6 feet (1.5–1.8 m) tall, a male black bear weighs 200 to 400 or more pounds (91–181 kg or more).

Like bears, wild pigs are intelligent and eat the same diet. Wild boars also dig up the ground to find roots to eat. The largest populations of wild boars live in the Appalachian Mountains and in the southern United States. The most-hunted wild pig is the razorback. Male wild pigs weigh up to 400 pounds (181 kg) or more. They have two large tusks (long, pointed teeth) projecting from the lower jaw that they use to dig for food or as weapons.

LOCATING HUNTING SPOTS

Hunters are responsible for finding a place to hunt big game. They may need to get reservations and permits to hunt on public lands and wildlife management areas. Wildlife managers and conservation officers can provide this information. These officials might know of farmers or ranchers who want hunters to reduce their big game population. Hunters can check the local assessor's office or county websites to find the owner of such a piece of land. Sometimes, members of a hunting group know of a private or public place. National forests are often open to big game hunters. The U.S. Forest Service administers these large blocks of public land.

Hunters must contact a landowner and ask permission to hunt on private land for a particular type of big game. Summer is the best time to contact landowners. Hunters should scout the land to get to know it and the wildlife living there. Studying the land with topographic and aerial maps increases a hunter's knowledge of where animals live.

SCOUTING IS NECESSARY

Big game hunters should scout their hunting area in advance of the season. If they are unfamiliar with an area, they may want to scout with an experienced hunter. By scouting, hunters become familiar with the land and can identify where to find the wildlife they want. Hunters look for changes in the habitat or population size. In particular, severe weather or shortages of food could cause big game populations to move to a new area.

Sometimes spotting big game is difficult. Hunters can look for other animal signs, such as game trails that go from cover (bedding or hiding place) to food or water. Deer, for instance,

Elk are social creatures that travel in herds, which are often led by a dominant male.

typically use the same trails. Hunters can examine animal tracks in the soil or snow. Large amounts of scat (animal droppings) in an area mean the animals have been eating or bedding there. Experienced hunters know what animals have been eating by looking at the nipped ends of grasses, twigs, or crops. Each type of big game animal has its own chew marks. Male deer during breeding season leave scrapes on the ground and rub marks on trees. These marks identify the location of the animals. Some hunters place camcorders in potential hunting areas to record wildlife movements. They watch the videos to determine the behavior of the animals and how many are in the area.

BE SAFE!

Being in good physical condition is important for a person so that he or she has an enjoyable hunt. Sometimes hunters walk long distances and carry heavy equipment. If they are not in good shape, hunters should start a regular exercise program at least two months before their planned hunt. An exercise program should include aerobic exercise, also called cardio or endurance activities. Aerobic exercise is physical activity that uses large muscle groups and increases the heart rate for a period of time. Examples include walking briskly, jogging, hiking, skiing, biking, or swimming laps. Sports such as basketball and football are also aerobic exercise.

Hunters need to plan for the unexpected and know how to survive in an emergency situation. They should always tell someone where they are going and when they expect to return. Don't scout or hunt alone. Outdoor skill is necessary for knowing how to build a fire and signal for help. Identifying one's location is also necessary.

WHEN EMERGENCIES HAPPEN

For emergencies, every hunter should carry a survival kit when scouting and hunting. Sporting stores sell survival packs. Hunters can make their own pack. A survival kit should contain a map of the area, a knife, a flashlight with working batteries, extra water and food, a compass, a whistle, and materials to start a fire, including waterproof matches. A large, thick garbage bag can provide the hunter with protection from cold, wind, snow, or rain. In addition, hunters should always bring a first aid kit. The type of first aid kit depends on the land, climate, and distance from a vehicle or cabin. Most kits contain bandages, tape, small scissors, aspirin or other pain relievers, tweezers, cotton swabs, and a first aid handbook. Sunblock and personal medicines should also go in a first aid kit. Taking a first aid course is a must for anyone who wishes to hunt.

ESSENTIAL EQUIPMENT

When scouting and hunting, people bring their survival and first aid kits and other useful items. Binoculars help them look for big game and identify legal big game animals. Experienced hunters carry a compass or use a global positioning system (GPS). They bring a phone for emergency calls.

Many states require hunters to wear blaze orange clothing so that other hunters can see them. Hunters might wear blaze orange vests and hats, even if they are not required by law to do so. Most archery hunters also wear camouflage clothing, which

Blaze orange hats, vests, and jackets help hunters stand out from the brush and wild animals.

helps to keep animals from seeing them in the woods. In cold weather, hunters dress warmly and in layers and wear hiking boots made of leather or rubber.

Hunters often bring sleeping bags to stay warm if they plan to be a long way from their vehicle. They might bring tents to provide shelter from wind and rain. Weather can change quickly and make hunting dangerous.

CHAPTER FOUR

HUNTING WAYS AND MEANS

N o two hunting trips—or hunting spots—are the same. In order to have a successful hunt, it's necessary to know multiple ways to approach the hunt. Many factors influence how a particular hunt is carried out, from how many hunters are in the group, to the types of weapons used, the weather, and the terrain.

MOVING OR STAYING PUT

Still or stationary hunting means silent hunting. Still hunters sneak through the woods to get close to big game. They move upward and into the wind and stop often so that they can surprise an animal without it seeing them. By slowly moving, still hunters keep alert for sights, sounds, or smells that mean big game is nearby. Animals watch for movement and sounds to signal danger, so they are less likely to spot hunters who are silent and stepping carefully. Still hunting works best when big game is bedded down or not active, typically during the middle of the day.

The way people still hunt is to take unhurried steps and stop. They slowly move only their heads and eyes to search the area for an animal, and repeat. Usually, big game hunters walk silent-

Bears are omnivores, like humans. They can eat both plants and meat—and honey as well.

ly for about five minutes and then wait and look in all directions for about five minutes. The best places to still hunt are in areas where animals live or frequent, like watering holes. Another place for still hunting is somewhere with a good food source nearby, such as a stand of oak trees with acorns or highbush cranberries.

All types of weapons can be used when still hunting. Although stationary hunting can be done any place, it is best done in thick woods and in shade. Animals are likely to notice glare off of faces and clothing in sunlight. No preparation is needed to still hunt, although a basic idea of where animals live is important. Moose hunters, for instance, can check the banks of streams for game trails leading to the water. People need to determine if the weather and wind are correct to still hunt. To keep animals from seeing them, hunters should not walk

Crossbows were first made by the Chinese sometime prior to the fourth century BCE. They made their way to Europe via Greek hunters.

across open areas. Usually still hunting is done by one person, but it works well with two people. The second hunter follows far behind the first.

STEALTH AND SNEAKING

Like still hunting, stalking requires excellent hunting skills. Hunters sneak up on big game without being detected. Although it is difficult to creep up within shooting range, experienced hunters can get less than one hundred feet (thirty meters) from an animal. To stalk, hunters follow a game trail to a bedded or feeding animal. Another method they use is they spot big game on a hill or mountainside and move toward it slowly. Bow hunters and rifle hunters stalk.

Hunters need to stay behind land formations and plants until they are close enough to shoot an animal. Walking hunting cannot be done effectively in thick woods because hunters cannot see their big game. Stalkers stay behind hills, trees, brush, tall crops or grass, or fencing so that an animal cannot see them. When hunting in open, flat land, stalkers often carry a clump of brush or weeds as cover. Stalking works well to hunt elk and black bears on mountainsides. Mule deer on high hills or in mountainous areas are also hunted in this way.

Most stalkers use binoculars to spot big game. Seeing an animal from a distance allows them to plan how and by what path they will stalk. After seeing an animal, hunters watch it closely for a few minutes. They try to determine whether it will stay in the same place. After stalking, an animal that is still feeding or lying down is usually close enough for a shot.

Walking hunting requires basic knowledge of the land and animal habitats. This method works well any time during the season. It does not require much advance preparation. An important skill that stalkers need is to accurately predict the weather. They must determine wind direction so that they can move upwind (wind in the face) without the animal smelling or hearing them. Experienced stalkers move only when an animal faces away from them or has its head down to feed or drink. They make sure that sunlight does not reflect off of their gun or scope. When they get close to their animal, they move as silently as possible until a successful shot can be made.

USING A STAND

Hunting from a tree stand is a popular way to pursue game. Hunters sit in stands above trees and brush to see into forest, bushes, or grass. They can look farther than if they were on the ground. A stand must offer a clear field of vision to shoot into. Stand hunting is used for any big game, particularly white-tailed deer and bear. This method is adaptable to both firearms and archery.

Although a stand can be a sturdy tree branch, most hunters use an elevated platform that is made in a tree or pulled up into a tree. The stand attaches to a limb or the trunk of a tree. Most stands hold one person. Big game should not be able to see a hunter in a stand.

Stand hunting can take some preparation time unless hunters know an area well. A few weeks before the season, hunters should carefully scout the land to find feeding, drinking, or bedding areas of the big game they want. After determining a place with many signs of wildlife activity, hunters select a tree and make their stand. Cautious animals often stay away from a new stand location for some time. During the season, hunters sit and wait in their stand for big game to pass by. Hunters might

Hunting stands are often sources of injury due to rotted wood, weak railings or steps, and slips by climbers.

sit for many hours. Stand hunting works best early, often before sunrise, or late in the day. During these times, animals move between feeding and resting places.

The wind is another important factor when choosing a site for a tree stand. Hunters build their tree stands downwind. This means that the wind is in the faces of hunters as they look at the area most likely to be used by the hunted animals. Most hunters have alternative stands for different wind conditions. Some use scent blockers to keep animals from smelling them. Animals will change their patterns of movement if an unusual scent, noise, or movement arises.

USING BAIT

In some states, baiting is a legal way to attract big game to a place for stand hunting. This method is very effective for white-tailed deer, bears, or wild boars. Baiting requires advance planning. Every day, hunters must put out food in an area in advance of the season. Good bait for deer is dried corn. Bears like candy, honey, cookies, and other sweets. Wild pigs eat any type of food. Over time, hunters note where big game enter the baiting place to feed. They will also see tracks of the animal. Hunters then build their tree stand near the feeding area and wait for the big game to come and feed. It is important to check what the law allows for baiting. For example, states typically restrict who can bait, when baiting is allowed, and the amount of food placed at feeding sites. Usually, bait must be a certain distance from trails, roads, or campsites used by the public.

HUNTING WITH A GROUP

Sometimes hunters use driving as a way to push or move animals out of their cover. To drive hunt, hunters line up and walk through woods or fields to move animals toward other hunters waiting nearby. This method is typically used by larger groups to hunt white-tailed deer or elk. Any firearm can be used for drives. However, group hunting is most effective with rifles because the animals are moving fast and sometimes are a long distance away. Animals responding to a drive are often moving too quickly for archers to make accurate shots. Some states allow dogs to be used as drivers when hunting for big game.

Depending on the situation, group hunting can work with a dozen or more hunters but usually is best with two to six people. Before the drive begins, people known as posters quietly move to positions at the end of the cover and stand still. Drivers spread out across the woods or fields. Usually, more drivers are needed than standers.

Because group hunting can be dangerous, safety rules are a priority. Beginners need to stay within arm's reach of experienced hunters. Another safety rule is that hunters must always know the positions of drivers and posters. No one should shoot when a hunter might be in the line of fire. Furthermore, all hunters must wear blaze orange clothing.

CHAPTER FIVE

THE NEXT STEPS

B agging a wild animal is not the end of a hunt, despite what a beginning hunter might think. Several other steps are necessary to complete a hunting trip successfully. Immediately after the death blow, hunters need to find the animal and dress it in the forest or field. Skinning and butchering can wait until the animal is transported back to camp or home. After the meat is divided up into smaller cuts, it is ready to be cooked and eaten.

FOLLOWING TRACKS

After hunters shoot at an animal, they determine if it was killed, wounded, or missed. Wounded big game often run some distance and must be tracked. They might run more than 100 yards (91 m), even when they are hit in the heart-lung area. Wounded large animals can be difficult to find because they may not show that they have been hit. If an animal is not seriously wounded, hunters usually wait thirty to sixty minutes before tracking it. During this waiting time, the animal will weaken from blood loss and lie down. However, during rain or snow, hunters often track wounded wildlife immediately so the tracks do not disappear.

Animals of North America
Plus animal tracks

animal tracks

Caribou

animal tracks

Elk

animal tracks

Musk-ox

animal tracks

Buffalo

Caribou are also known as reindeer. The elk shown here is called a moose in America and an elk in British English.

To track, hunters note where the big game was hit. They mark the spot with a piece of clothing or colored survey tape or use a landmark, such as a tree or rock. Then they quickly and quietly follow the blood trail. If hunters cannot see blood, they look in widening circles for signs from where the animal was shot. Signs of a shot might be drops of blood, hair, fragments of bone, or unusual tracks of the animal. Tracking is easiest with two or more hunters. If they cannot find the animal, hunters return to their starting point and try a second time.

IN THE FIELD

Once big game is harvested, hunters must get to their animal. They carefully approach a shot animal from behind. A shot that is well placed can kill an animal instantly. If the shot is not well aimed, the animal might be stunned and could seriously harm a hunter by lashing out with its sharp hooves, antlers, claws, or tusks. Hunters must keep their weapons ready for a second shot as they approach a downed animal.

Next is field dressing, or butchering. This step is key to cool the animal quickly, which preserves the meat. Wearing latex gloves, hunters cut open the body cavity with a sharp knife. They

remove the windpipe, stomach, intestines, and all other organs. Some people wipe out the cavity with dry grass or with a cloth.

Hunters must follow the regulations of the state and license tag their harvested animal. Tagging means punching the day and month of the kill on a tag and attaching it to the animal.

There are an estimated thirty million deer in the United States. The Insurance Institute for Highway Safety has found that vehicle collisions with deer result in about two hundred deaths annually.

If allowed by law, hunters prefer to attach the tag after field dressing and dragging, so that the tag does not get ripped off during this process. Hunters may need to transport the animal to a registration and checking station to receive a permanent possession tag.

Wild boars do not taste exactly like domestic pigs, though they are similar species. Instead, boar meat tastes like a cross between beef and pork.

To transport the harvested animal home or to a station, hunters tie rope around the neck or antlers and wrap the rope around the animal's muzzle or snout. Then they haul, usually by dragging, the animal out of the woods or brush. Often more than one hunter pulls because a harvested big game animal typically weighs more than 100 pounds (45 kg). Dragging on snow usually does little damage to the animal's fur. Dragging on bare ground can ruin the hide, so hunters must carefully pull or carry the animal out of the woods. Hunters hoist the harvested animal on top of their vehicle or into a trailer, cover it with a tarp, and tie the animal down.

USING GAME

Some hunters bring the carcass (harvested animal) to professional butchers, who prepare the meat for eating. If hunters butcher their animal, they must follow safe methods. To begin the process, they remove the hide from the carcass right away. Next, they cut off the neck, saw the animal in half, and cut the halves into smaller sections of steaks and roasts. Many hunters age their big game meat at 42 degrees Fahrenheit (5.5 degrees Celsius) because it becomes tender and tastes better. Aging is often done by keeping the large sections cool and dry for a week or more. One way to do this is to wrap the large sections in a cotton sack and hang them in a cool garage or shed. After aging, the meat is ready to be cut into smaller pieces for cooking or freezing.

Big game meat is tasty and nutritious! Some hunters enjoy learning how to cook wild meat. It can be prepared in many healthy ways, such as in soups, stews, stir-frys, and as jerky, steaks, or roasts. Big game meat is lean and lower in fat and calories than beef. If a wild boar is harvested, some people roast the entire carcass on a spit and invite friends over for a party.

To keep the memory of a good hunt, hunters might take photographs or videos of their harvest to share with family,

TANNING YOUR HIDES

Some hunters tan their big game hide to use as a rug or blanket or to make warm clothing. Another use is to hang it above a fireplace or on a wall. Tanning is not difficult to do, but it takes time. Instead of tanning at home, many hunters take their hide to taxidermists. If hunters cannot use their hides, they can donate them at drop-off sites. Some states have hides-for-habitat programs. Hunters donate deer hides to these programs. The hides are sold, and the money goes to habitat projects throughout the state, wildlife research, and educational programs for children and teens. The Benevolent and Protective Order of Elks, a national organization, has an annual drive to collect deer, elk, and other animal hides to benefit disabled war veterans. The hides are sold, and the money is donated to veteran's hospitals. Alternatively, veterans can use the hides for craft kits to make purses, wallets, moccasins, gloves, and clothes.

friends, and other hunters. They can take photos in the woods or field or at home. Some hunters use the antlers of their big game as coat racks or in artwork. They might mount the antlers on a wall as a display.

Some hunters want the head of their big game as a trophy. Taxidermists are professionals who mount big game trophies. They start by covering a premade foam model of the animal with special glue. Then they carefully stretch and fit the tanned hide of the big game on the model and add glass eyes. After the glue dries, the trophy is ready to mount on a wall.

WHAT TO DO THE NEXT TIME

Preparation for the next hunt begins as soon as hunters come home. They clean their weapons and other equipment and wash their dirty clothes. They sharpen and oil their knives and take the batteries out of headlights and flashlights. Anything used in hunting that is broken should be replaced. If hunting clothing or equipment is needed, hunters watch for off-season sales to buy them. All items are then packed for the next hunt.

Many hunters keep a journal of their hunts, making notes of everything interesting that happened. They can keep a journal by hand or in an electronic document. They also need to remember to map where they hunted. They can go to the website of the state nature resources department or to Google Earth to make a map or mark a paper map.

Hunters can learn more about hunting and big game in numerous ways. Many join local hunting and sporting clubs. They can take classes at the clubs and share information on local big game populations and hunting. They can research hunting techniques and big game through books, magazines, and the internet.

Many state and national organizations offer teen hunter programs. These events are often at local sporting clubs and schools. Some events test hunter knowledge and shooting and other skills. The National Rifle Association holds the Youth Hunter Education Challenge program. Teen hunters compete in contests of outdoor weapon shooting of game animal targets under real field conditions. They can also take a written test about hunting ethics and safety issues. The National 4-H Council offers a Shooting Sports program. Some nature centers and community education programs provide courses in survival skills and compass orientation. First aid courses are available through local American Red Cross chapters.

Hunters might not harvest an animal during every hunt. Each hunt, however, provides hunters with a healthy outdoor experience and practice. They improve their knowledge of safety precautions and hunting skills and big game habitat and behavior. Good hunters stay up to date with laws and regulations because these can change. Big game hunting provides challenging and exciting memories that will last a lifetime. Moreover, it gives hunters the chance to eat delicious meals of big game meat.

GLOSSARY

aerial Carried out from the air, particularly using aircraft, as in aerial photography of a region.

ammunition Bullets and gunpowder used in firearms.

antlers Bony structures that quickly develop from bone pads or lumps on the head of a male deer, moose, or elk. Antlers are shed after the breeding season.

archery The skill of shooting with a bow and arrow.

bait Food used to lure wild game to within shooting range.

barrel The metal tube of a rifle.

bedding area The sleeping area of an animal.

black powder An explosive mixture used as a propellant in muzzleloaders.

butcher To process an animal's meat into usable sizes.

caliber The inside diameter of the barrel of a rifle or the diameter of a bullet.

camaraderie Trust and friendship between people who spend time together.

camouflage Anything that conceals a person or equipment by making them appear to be part of the natural surroundings.

conservation Protection and preservation of nature.

endangered An animal population in such small numbers that it is in danger of becoming extinct.

extinction No longer existing.

field dressing Preparing a recently harvested animal so that its body temperature lowers and the meat stays fresh.

game Wild animals hunted for food or sport.

global positioning system (GPS) Handheld computers that can calculate an exact position using a global positioning satellite.

habitat The area or environment where an animal lives.

harvest The act of shooting and recovering an animal.

hide The skin of an animal.

illegal Against the law.

muzzle The open end of a gun barrel.

poaching Hunting game in a forbidden area or hunting animals that are illegal to take.

safety A device on a firearm that keeps it from being fired.

scope A small telescope on a rifle barrel.

season The length of time to hunt specific game.

slug A lead bullet used in shotguns.

stand hunting A type of hunting in which a hunter uses a tree stand, an elevated platform, or ground blind or natural cover to wait for the game to appear.

target Something that is shot at with firearms or bow and arrow.

topographic Relating to the accurate representation of the physical features of an area.

tracking Following an animal.

trespass To unlawfully enter a person's property.

Canadian Firearms Program
RCMP National Headquarters
Headquarters Building
73 Leikin Drive
Ottawa ON KIA 0R2
Canada
(800) 731-4000
Website: http://www.rcmp-grc.gc.ca/cfp-pcaf/index-eng.htm
This organization provides information on firearm licensing, registration, and safety training across Canada.

Dominion of Canada Rifle Association
45 Shirley Boulevard
Nepean ON K2K 2W6
Canada
(613) 829-8281
Website: http://www.dcra.ca
Facebook: @TheDCRA
This group supports the safe handling of firearms and the sport of shooting throughout Canada.

National Rifle Association of America (NRA)
11250 Waples Mill Road
Fairfax, VA 22030
(800) 672-3888
Website: https://firearmtraining.nra.org
Facebook and Instagram: @NationalRifleAssociation
Twitter: @NRA
The NRA offers a number of programs to teach shooters safe, ethical, and responsible firearm practices.

Parks Canada National Office
30 Victoria Street
Gatineau, Quebec J8X 0B3
Canada
(888) 773-8888
Website: https://www.pc.gc.ca/en
Facebook and Twitter: @ParksCanada
Instagram: @parks.canada
This government agency is committed to protecting both the
    natural and cultural heritage of Canada's wilderness and
    territory in a way that ensures the health of both human and
    animal species.

Rocky Mountain Elk Foundation
5705 Grant Creek
Missoula, MT 59808
(406) 523-4500
Website: http://www.rmef.org
Facebook: @RMEF1
Twitter: @RMEF
This foundation works to ensure the future of elk and other wild-
    life, their habitats, and hunting heritage by sponsoring chap-
    ters across the country as well as providing education about
    large North American mammals.

US Department of Agriculture Forest Service
Attn: Office of Communication
Mailstop: 1111
1400 Independence Avenue SW
Washington, DC 20250-1111
(800) 832-1355
Website: http://www.fs.fed.us
Facebook: @USForestService

Twitter: @forestservice
Instagram: @u.s.forestservice
An agency of the US Department of Agriculture, the Forest Service manages and maintains millions of acres of public lands in
national forests and grasslands.

U.S. Fish & Wildlife Service
1849 C Street NW
Washington, DC 20240
(800) 344-9453
Website: http://www.fws.gov
Facebook, Twitter, and Instagram: @usfws
This government agency manages US natural resources in order to
conserve, protect, and enhance wildlife, plants, and their habitats.

FOR FURTHER READING

Carpenter, Tom. *Bear Hunting*. Minneapolis, MN: Abdo Publishing, 2016.

Carpenter, Tom. *Deer Hunting*. Mendota, MN: Focus Readers, 2017.

Gaspar, Joe, and Jack Weaver. *Hunting*. New York, NY: Rosen Publishing, 2016.

Hanson, Jonathan, and Roseann Beggy Hanson. *Animal Tracks*. Helena, MT: FalconGuides, 2016.

Hemstock, Annie. *Bow Hunting*. New York, NY: Rosen Publishing, 2015.

Hemstock, Annie. *Hunting Laws and Safety*. New York, NY: Rosen Publishing, 2015.

Meyer, Susan. *Hunting Dogs: Different Breeds and Special Purposes*. New York, NY: Rosen Publishing, 2013.

Sparano, Vin T. *The Greatest Hunting Stories Ever Told: Classic Tales of Hunting Grizzly, Moose, Cape Buffalo, and Much More*. New York, NY: Skyhorse Publishing, 2015.

Wood, Alix. *Hunting on the Map*. New York, NY: PowerKids Press, 2015.

BIBLIOGRAPHY

Baird, Joel Banner. "Hunters as Environmental Stewards." *Burlington Free Press*, November 29, 2009. http://www .burlingtonfreepress.com/article/20091129 /LIVING09/91125050/Hunters-as-environmental-stewards.

Boddington, Craig. *Fair Chase in North America*. Missoula, MT: Boone & Crockett Club, 2004.

Boddington, Craig. *The Perfect Shot, North America: Shot Placement for North American Big Game*. Huntington Beach, CA: Safari Press, 2006.

Coor, Sam. "Hunters with Drive." *Duluth News Tribune,* November 22, 2009. pp. E1, E3.

Creative Publishing. *The Complete Guide to Hunting*. Chanhassen, MN: Creative Publishing, 1999.

Creative Publishing. *Dressing and Cooking Wild Game*. Chanhassen, MN: Creative Publishing, 2000.

Creative Publishing. *Hunting in North America*. Chanhassen, MN: Creative Publishing, 2000.

Farrell, Sean Patrick. "The Urban Deerslayer." *New York Times,* November 24, 2009. http://www.nytimes.com/2009/11/25 /dining/25hunt.html.

Fischl, Josef, and Leonard Lee Rue III. *After Your Deer Is Down: The Care and Handling of Big Game*. Tulsa, OK: Winchester Press, 1981.

Kalthoff, Ken. "Hunters to Bring Not-So-Little Piggies to Market." NBC Channel 5 Dallas-Fort Worth, January 20, 2010. http:// www.nbcdfw.com/news/local-beat/Wild-Hogs-Run -Rampant-in-Texas-82219607.html.

Lund, Duane R. *A Beginner's Guide to Hunting and Trapping Secrets*. Cambridge, MN: Adventure Publications, 1988.

Maas, David R. *North American Game Animals*. Minnetonka, MN: Cy Decosse, 1995.

Meili, Launi. *Rifle: Steps to Success.* Champaign, IL: Human Kinetics, 2008.

National Shooting Sports Foundation. "The Ethical Hunter." Pamphlet, 2006.

National Shooting Sports Foundation. "Firearms Safety Depends on You." Pamphlet, 2006.

National Shooting Sports Foundation. "The Hunter and Conservation." Booklet, 2006.

Petersen's Hunting. *Petersen's Hunting Guide to Big Game.* New York, NY: Skyhorse Publishing, 2016.

Peterson, David H. (Hunter Education Instructor, Two Harbors, MN) Interview. January 2010.

Petzal, David E., ed. *The Experts' Book of Big Game Hunting in North America.* New York, NY: Cord Communications Corporation, 1976.

O'Connor, Jack. *The Art of Hunting Big Game in North America.* New York, NY: Outdoor Life, 1967.

Outdoor Empire. *Minnesota Firearms Safety Hunter Education, Student Manual.* Seattle, WA: Outdoor Empire Publishing, 2001.

Rinella, Steven. *The Complete Guide to Hunting, Butchering, and Cooking Wild Game. Volume 1, Big Game.* New York, NY: Spiegel & Grau, 2015.

Rupp, J. Scott. *RifleShooter Magazine's Guide to Big Game Hunting.* New York, NY: Skyhorse Publishing, 2017.

INDEX

A

aging, of meat, 49, 50
ammunition, 8, 11
antlers, 49
  danger of, 46
  shedding of, 27
  as trophies, 51
archers, 14, 15, 43
archery, 7, 9, 40
  classes in, 9
  equipment, 21, 33–34
arrows, 8, 9, 14, 15, 16

B

bait
  illegal, 22
  legal, 22, 42
barrel, 13, 14
bear, 4, 19–20, 21, 26, 29–30, 39,
  40, 42
bedding areas, 40
binoculars, 33, 39
black powder guns, 14
blaze orange clothing, 33, 43
boar, wild, 4, 19–20, 21, 25, 29–30,
  42, 50
bows, 8, 9
  hunting with, 14–16, 39
butchering, 44, 46, 49

C

caliber

of a bullet, 13
of a rifle, 11, 13, 14
camaraderie, 6
camouflage clothing, 33–34
conservation, 6–7, 17, 19, 24–25
  clubs, 8–9
  officers, 30
  state department of, 8

D

deserts, 4, 27
drive hunting, 43

E

education, hunting, 8–10, 19, 24,
  50, 52
elk, 4, 19–20, 21, 26, 27, 29, 39,
  43, 50
emergencies, 32, 33
endangered animals, 7, 25
ethics, and hunting, 21, 52
extinction, 25

F

field dressing, 46, 48
firearm safety, 9
first aid kits, 33
foothills, 4
forests, 4, 8, 26, 29, 40, 44
  edges of, 27
  national and state, 18, 30

ABOUT THE AUTHORS

Xina M. Uhl has written numerous educational books for young people, in addition to textbooks, teacher's guides, lessons, and assessment questions. She has tackled subjects including sports, history, biographies, technology, and health concerns. Although she has friends and family who hunt, she shoots animals only through her camera lens. Her blog details her publications as well as interesting facts and the occasional cat picture.

Judy Monroe Peterson is married to an avid hunter who has more than fifty years of hunting experience. She has earned two master's degrees and is the author of many educational books for young people. Currently, she is a writer and editor of K–12 and post–high school curriculum materials on a variety of subjects, including biology, life science, and the environment.

ABOUT THE CONSULTANT

Benjamin Cowan has over twenty years of both big game and small game hunting experience. In addition to being an avid hunter, Cowan is also a member of many conservation organizations. He currently resides in west Tennessee.

PHOTO CREDITS